# *Daffodils in December*

### Poems from an Unexpected Life

Alice Bingham Gorman

Fleur-de-Lis Press
Louisville, Kentucky
2025

Copyright © 2025 Alice Bingham Gorman

All rights reserved. No part of this book may be reproduced in any form or by any electronic or mechanical means including information storage and retrieval systems without permission in writing from the author, except by a reviewer who may quote brief passages in a review. Please direct requests to Fleur-de-Lis Press, 1436 St. James Court, #1, Louisville, Kentucky 40208.

Book design: Jonathan Weinert
Front cover graphic: Haley Manin Ott
Author photo: Patricia Christakos

Printed in the United States of America
First Edition

*Library of Congress Cataloging-in-Publication Data*
Names: Gorman, Alice Bingham, author.
Title: Daffodils in december: poems from an unexpected life / Alice Bingham Gorman.
Description: Louisville: Fleur-de-Lis Press, 2025.
Identifiers: LCCN 2025904157 | ISBN 9798218628543
Subjects: LCGFT: Poetry

Fleur-de-Lis Press of The Louisville Review Corporation
1436 St. James Court, #1
Louisville, Kentucky 40208

www.louisvillereview.org

# Praise for *Daffodils in December*

Anaïs Nin noted, "We write to taste life twice, in the moment and in retrospect." That's precisely what Alice Gorman undertakes and accomplishes in her collection, *Daffodils in December*. Heartful and genuine, these poems collectively and consciously render the earned wisdom and joys of a life well-worth living with all its emotional complexities. A book for anyone who has ever asked the proverbial question of life's meaning. Gorman answers this insightfully and wittingly for herself and for us.

—**Richard Blanco**
2013 Presidential Inaugural Poet and author of *Homeland of My Body*

Lively and smart, with unexpected metaphors and a beautifully relaxed voice, surprise images abound in Alice Gorman's wonderful collection, *Daffodils in December*. "A colorless stone in a tight fitted wall" unlocks a world—though Gorman herself is hardly a colorless stone of a poet. Her portraits are electric: the poet's mother becomes the Queen who heard three conversations at once. A granddaughter's lovely face has a "calyx" mouth. And she is a splendid quick sketch artist whose love story infuses all these poems with freshness, particularly the tender, vulnerable "A Love Lesson." May this candid, lyrical book of poems sail.

—**Molly Peacock**
Author of *The Widow's Crayon Box*

"Joy and woe are woven fine," wrote William Blake, who makes a brief appearance in Alice Gorman's lovely chapbook *Daffodils in December*. Blake's line perfectly fits this collection, which traces a life's journey through joys and sorrows that are never fully separable. It is the speaker's ongoing struggle to understand these interwoven complexities that animates these poems. And it is her commitment, from a very early age, to the imagination, the spirit, and love, that helps to guide her through doubts, guilt, and grief, leaving open, through it all, "the gift of possibility."

—**Jeffrey Harrison**
Author of *Between Lakes*

# Contents

*Foreword*     v

| | |
|---|---|
| Daffodils in December | 3 |
| Learning Stages | 4 |
| Identity Dreams | 6 |
| My Father's Words | 7 |
| Visions of My Mother | 8 |
| Southern Cross | 10 |
| Beyond Choice | 14 |
| Empty Pool | 17 |
| Requiem for a Marriage | 18 |
| What Matters | 19 |
| A Widow's Valentine | 20 |
| When It's Over | 22 |
| Reflection | 23 |
| Learning to Dance Alone | 24 |
| In the Eventide | 25 |
| My Name | 26 |
| The House of Eighty | 28 |
| A Poem Comes | 29 |

| | |
|---|---|
| My Granddaughter at Twelve | 30 |
| A Love Lesson | 31 |
| On the Verge | 33 |
| A New Galaxy | 34 |
| Fate | 36 |
| To Love Again | 37 |
| Gratitude | 39 |
| Credo | 41 |
| *Acknowledgments* | 42 |
| *About the Author* | 44 |
| *About Fleur-de-Lis Press* | 45 |

# Foreword

Alice Gorman's beautifully and carefully crafted poems take me from the poet's early childhood to her eighties. Here is a familiar image or scene, yet it has become fresh and full of new meaning—shared with me. The unafraid intimacy of these poems reassures us—we are all right, we have even become more intact than we were before because we see more clearly. And we are less alone.

The poet's vision is clear and bright because it acknowledges what is real—in both the harsher outer world of fact and in our secret tender hearts. The clarity and accessible nature of Alice Gorman's poems sometimes make me feel as though I'm reading Emily Dickinson.

Alice Gorman's world is a balanced world: sorrow and loss are met by joy and resilience or simple memory. What is inevitable is acknowledged: "What's left is silence / the howling sound / of silence / an empty space once filled / with the soft music / of breath."

And Alice's world is capacious enough to hold both hope—"Might our stars align in a new galaxy?"—but also to pause in recognition of what is, "without asking for more."

These are wonderful poems both tender and tough, always enjoying the light, not fearful of the dark.

—**Sena Jeter Naslund**
Author of *Ahab's Wife*, *Four Spirits*, and *The Fountain of Saint James Court, or Portrait of the Artist as an Old Woman*
Founding Editor of *The Louisville Review* and Fleur-de-Lis Press

*for* David

I have walked through many lives,
some of them my own,

*Stanley Kunitz*

# Daffodils in December

Impossible, you say,
but I stand firm.
I hear the voices
call me:

A burst of yellow trumpets
blowing the defiance
of spring
into the bassoon mouth
of winter.
Slender green stems,
clarions of the spirit
ringing bells
of recognition.

Madness, you say,
as you turn away.
Yet here I am—
alive with expectation.

# Learning Stages

At four years old,
impatient with lagging grownups,
I decided to drive
my grandmother's big black Packard.
After lunging my small foot
onto the pedal,
I lurched into a tree.
My mother, who always
adhered to the rules,
punished me
for my reckless behavior.
My grandmother, who never
learned to drive,
praised me
for my courage.

Within the protection
of a white picket fence
and a wide green lawn,
as an only child,
the world was mine.
I climbed in mimosa branches,
hollowed a space
under a weeping willow
for my imaginary friends,
*Fansen* and *Murphreesboro*.
Once my sister Kate was born,

my friends disappeared.
I was no longer alone.

At age fourteen
in the state of Tennessee,
I had a learner's permit and
a maroon Morris Minor,
an English convertible
with a slow speed governor.
(My father's idea of safety).
That car took me to the drugstore
for a chocolate soda and comic books,
Brenda Starr and Rex Morgan MD,
over country roads, even across
the Mississippi bridge to Arkansas.
How I loved the freedom!

# Identity Dreams

Once I dreamed
I was an otter,
a small playful being
as much at home romping
with friends on the beach
as floating alone on the sea,
non-threatening, non-predatory,
fun loving and free—
I knew I was loved
for just being me.

Suppose I had dreamed
I was a snake,
a slithery creature with a rattle
and fangs, or a buzzard,
a scavenger, a carrion feeder,
or a fat hairy spider
hiding in a tree—
I'd be feared and loathed
for just being me.

# My Father's Words

How sadly I recall
my father's words, those
epithets spoken at night,

words like *nigger*
and *commie*
and *wop*, words

that fell like bombs upon
the innocent ground of
my childhood mind, words

so different
from his daylight advice,
his humanity and wisdom
unaltered by alcohol:

*Count your blessings!*
*Do your best!*
*Walk in another's shoes!*
*Read Dickens and Blake!*
*Learn "Tyger, Tyger*
*burning bright . . ."*

words that still resonate
in my adult mind
but fail to efface
those other words.

# Visions of My Mother

For so many years,
her effulgent blue eyes
lit up the room,
captivating strangers,
reaffirming friends,
her percipient ears could discern
three conversations at once,
her queenly bearing
ruled the house.

Towards the end,
her wispy hair,
her feathery legs,
the blue-black bruises
covering skin over bone,
the curve of her back
bridging the hollow
of her sunken breast,
her sighs of despair
revealed her defeat.

Finally, after ninety-five years
of gracing the world
with her satin charm,
its painful warp
and pleasured weft,
so artfully woven

throughout her life,
she is peacefully buried
in the soft cotton of time.

# Southern Cross

It isn't the food
I've left behind:
sliced ripe tomatoes, white corn
off the cob with bits of green pepper,
turnip greens cooked to death
with fat back and salt,
barbequed pork ribs,
dripping Tabasco and catsup,
chicken drumsticks lifted
from hot bacon grease
in a black iron skillet,
cornbread without sugar,
served with Sunday dinner.

It isn't the spring:
the piney woods briefly laced
with dogwood and azaleas,
a flow of yellow daffodils
crisscrossing green lawns,
the juxtaposition of forsythia,
wisteria and pussy willow,
the roar of John Deere
plowing fields for cotton
and tobacco and grain,
daylight lingering
longer into night.

It isn't the summer:
the June aroma of magnolias,
creeping jasmine and gardenias,
fireflies flickering
through their milk bottle prisons,
metal chains creaking
on the back porch swing,
attic fans thrumming,
pulling freshness and cool
into airless bedrooms at night.

It isn't the music:
the wail of the blues,
the shimmer of strings
from B.B. King's "Lucille,"
the beat of Jerry Lee,
his feet on the piano,
the swivel hips of Elvis
in his blue suede shoes,
the fire in his voice
that ignited the world.

I've left behind:
cracked concrete and broken windows
in abandoned urban schools,
chickens poking and pecking
at the scorched August earth,

yard dogs baring yellowed teeth
to deter drug-addicts
from stealing the lone TV
in a three-room fatherless shack,
old jacked-up cars left to rust
in kudzu-covered ditches,
a breach too wide
for all but a few
to reach the other side.

I've left behind:
a line of shiny SUV's
and endowed gymnasiums
in white flight schools,
gated communities with armed guards
protecting possessions
of people professing love
in Sunday pews,
then voting against it
in every election,
ladies at cocktail parties
in urgent conversation
about the Club and the Help,
a vise of voices
squeezing my breath away.

I had to leave, but
I will never be gone
from all that I loved, or
from the guilt I bear
for my years
of silence.

# Beyond Choice

Suppose I had been lucky enough
to live with my choices,
instead of my agonizing disappointments.
I would have attended
Vassar College
instead of Bennett Jr. College,
once called a *finishing school.*

Imagine my life
had I been accepted at Vassar,
an average student, one among many.
As it turned out,
I was a star at the *finishing school,*
an honors student, winner of
The Humanities Award, The Bennett Medallion.
My art history classes inspired a career,
a creative writing course
led to publishing a novel.

Suppose I had won the competition
for The Maid of Cotton,
a singular honor for a southern woman.
I would have been on a plane
the very next day,
beginning the adventure of lifetime,
a chance to travel the world
as an ambassador of cotton,

I would have missed the arrival
of the man of my dreams,
a Yale graduate from
an illustrious Connecticut family,
a dancer, a skier, a charmer,
the man I would agree to marry,
a Cathedral wedding,
three children who've added
the most valuable dimension
to my life.

Suppose I had stayed married
after twenty years, instead of
accepting divorce—
his choice, not mine.

Imagine spending my remaining years
as an unloved wife,
living an existence prescribed
by generations before me,
I might have improved my tennis score,
mastered the game of bridge,
perhaps become a consumate hostess,
a more valuable board member.

I would never have discovered
my creative life,

owned a contemporary art gallery
on 57th street in New York City,
earned a master's degree in Writing,
recognized the heart of who I am,
experienced unimagineable joy
and painful losses,
known the true meaning of love.

# Empty Pool

While standing midstream
I asked,
do you love me?
You said no.

I blinked
at my dreams
bobbing in the ripples,
disappearing downstream.

I reeled
in the line I had
cast out to you,
the line lying slack
in a pool of still water.

I turned and headed
toward the other bank,
grieving for the life
we would never share,

for the person I realized
was never there.

# Requiem for a Marriage

This marriage is dead.

Let us celebrate!
> With chorus,
> soloists and symphony,
> let us herald
> the rise of the Spirit,
> as we mourn
> the loss of a dream.

How could it be?
> It was blessed by God
> in his most honored house.
> It was vowed by his children
> "Until death do us part."
> It was witnessed by hundreds
> who pledged their support.

But the facts are clear:
> This marriage is dead.
> The body of commitment
> lies rigid and cold,
> the breath of unity, gone.

Let us celebrate!

# What Matters

I wake with the light
of gratitude and curiosity,
the determination
to celebrate every day!

To be open to the possible,
the new and untried,
to be willing to fail
again and again,

to let go of the guilt
for things left undone,
for opportunities missed,
for harsh judgements passed.

I revel in the music
of spontaneous laughter,
the simple joy of the words
*I love you.*

# A Widow's Valentine

I miss being two
instead of one,
those simple things
that defined our shared life:
   sipping a Chardonnay
   on a sunset porch,
   visiting the Farmer's Market
   to discover a new cheese,
   spending the weekend in Quebec
   at the Frontenac Hotel
   where we slept late
   and never answered the phone.

On the darkest days I miss
the promises we made:
   we would grow gray together,
   ignore wrinkles and sag.
   You would take my hand
   in the land of infirmity,
   be my eyes and ears,
   or I would be yours.

As the years fade away,
certain memories rise
with greater meaning:
   your laugh that could crack
   a crystal glass,
   your nimble wit

that never wounded,
your squabbling over directions
to a well-known destination,
your snore that woke me
from deepest sleep,
your joy over breakfast
of kidney stew that reeked,
your disdain for men's fashion
and for those who complied,
your strange superstitions
like no hats on a bed,

your morning chair
cluttered with newspapers
and books,
those quiet times,
doing absolutely nothing
together.

# When It's Over

When it's over
time stops
The hours no longer matter
No more pills, no needles
no anxious hovering
no tormenting speculation

Gone are the days
the endless weeks
maybe months, or years
of watching and waiting

What's left is silence
the howling sound
of silence
an empty space once filled
with the soft music
of breath

# Reflection

Without you, your presence
your benevolent reflection,
how do I know
I am still desirable and true?

How do I know
if my eyes are seductive
they speak
without words?

Without your smile
your loving laughter
how do I know
if I am accepted
for all that I am?

I know this—
Even if you were still here,
I must learn to honor myself,
to see as the blind see,
to hold a mirror
to my own reflection.

# Learning to Dance Alone

Turn on the music,
a sound that ignites
your desire to dance.
Feel the beat in your bones,
in your muscles, in your memory
until your fingers want to snap,
your feet want to move,
and before you know it,
you are up, off of your couch,
out of your solitary life.

You are dancing barefoot
to calypso in Bermuda,
doing a fox trot or a rhumba,
at a Long Island debut party
wearing a strapless taffeta dress.
You are waltzing
at your first wedding,
feeling the joy of the moment,
believing the dance
will never end.

Then abruptly you awaken
to a dawn of silence,
the music stopped,
no partner in sight,
your arms in the air.

# In the Eventide

There are days
in the eventide of my life
when my mind wanders,
a searcher with an empty cup,
not asking for coins
or bread, more in hopes of
affirmation, a published poem,
an invitation to participate,
a currency of proof
that I am worthy.

Days pass
without acknowledgement
that my existence matters.
Am I a peacock feather
amid a fan of others?
A colorless stone
in a tight-fitted wall?
Or am I simply a human
slowly learning to trust
my cup is unique
and full enough.

# My Name

In the dream
a stranger asks my name—
a simple request
but I cannot answer.
I cannot remember my name.

Is my name daughter?
My duty name,
a genetic composite
of all that came before me,
all I carry within me.

Is my name mother?
I hear a call, a plaintive call—
I reach my arms towards
those disappearing, those
answering calls
no longer meant for me.

Is my name wife?
My name once linked,
a name divorced,
a name twice buried.

Is my name girl?
That lanky reed, that willow bough,
that tremulous longing for more.

Is my name woman?
As in the painting the artist named
*Woman on a High Wall.*

> She stands
> a thousand steps up
> on a precarious perch,
> long shadows falling
> from the archways below,
> with steel in her spine,
> a solid stance,
> a knowing expression on her face.

I look in her eyes
and remember my name.

# The House of Eighty

From this threshold,
where I stand firm,
I wonder

if I am visible
through the windows
of my eyes.

Can you see
the many rooms?
Can you tell

that nothing
has been lost,
nearly everything

has been used,
and a few things
transformed?

Do you see
the light in my living room
still shines—

and I am still at home?

# A Poem Comes

A poem comes
unbidden, a surprise,
an irrepressible

feeling, a sensation,
a demand to be
acknowledged, an idea

in need of words,
an image, a metaphor,
a way to emerge

from an experience
of pain or joy, a way
to be transformed.

# My Granddaughter at Twelve

She descended the stairs
from the chrysalis of her room,
a pink strapless dress

barely covered her curves,
crimson lipstick shimmered
on the calyx of her mouth,

black mascara magnified
the expectation in her eyes,
two-inch heels announced

her discarded youth, except
for a blonde ponytail,
bouncing behind her head.

# A Love Lesson

My grandson touches the wrinkles
on my face, looks wistfully into my eyes
and whispers, *Are you still alive?*
*Your skin feels so old. Can you still play*
*and have fun? Do you look forward*
*to summer—and your birthday?*

*Oh yes*, I tell him, a smile
on my eighty-year-old lips,
a warmth rising in my body.
*I am alive! I can play and have fun.*
*I look forward to every day.*
I can't tell him how his life will be,
all he may have to endure
to still be alive when he is old.

I can tell him my secret, my belief in love.
I can share the joys I thought
would never end,
the sorrows I feared
I could not bear, the bloom of passion
within my youthful body, the garden of pleasures
through my middle years,
my love of Verdi and Vermeer, of
Dickinson and Yeats, creative memories
that cannot be taken away,
memories that kept my heart open
for another to enter, another with memories

of his own joys and pain,
a person who kept his belief in love,
kept his heart open
for me.

# On the Verge

You know the feeling—
that flutter of awareness
expanding your heart,
that sense of stepping off
into the vast unknown.

You know you are facing
a life-altering choice.
Should you trust your instinct?
Surrender your control?
Risk losing yourself
before you find life anew?

Yet, if you refuse,
you will have rejected
the gift of possibility,
abandoned the path
that led you to know
you were on the verge.

# A New Galaxy

Here are my thoughts
about the stars
and the world around me.

>about the seasons,
>>the luscious taste of summer tomatoes
>>the sound of silence from winter snow
>>the intoxicating scent of lilacs in spring

>about artists,
>>Picasso's switch from soft Blue to hard cubism
>>the dreaminess of O'Keefe's flowers and clouds
>>the playfulness of Chagall's lovers floating in space

>about history,
>>the tragedy of man's drive for power
>>the massacres of innocence
>>Auschwitz, Nagasaki, My Lai, and Gaza

>about religion,
>>how I see Spirit in everything,
>>believe what cannot be known,
>>accept Love as the Force.

Each thought is a star
in the galaxy of my life,
>>the colors, shapes, angles, and curves
>>formed through time and trial

        by parents and siblings
        order of birth
        mentors and friends
        choices and decisions
        cosmic coincidence.

Might our stars align
in a new galaxy?

# Fate

Throughout the many stages
of my eighty-one years
were you always there?

Invisible to the eye,
not fully formed,
more a belief
in what could be,

two souls
linked in space,
drawn together
by a magnetic force,

two people
whose prophetic parallel past
would lead them to each other.

# To Love Again

Suppose we had never met?
Would you have found someone else?
I think so.
You're a man who's known love,
a man who needs a woman,
the comfort of her body,
the challenge of her mind,
the joys of a shared life.
A widower for the second time,
you would not have remained alone.

How is it that you chose me?
An independent woman,
a divorcee once, a widow twice,
by all appearances content in my life.
How did you see my secret heart,
my romantic nature?
How did you recognize my dream—
that someday, someway,
I would fall in love again?

If we had never met
would I have found someone else?
I don't think so.
After sixteen years
of happily living alone,
I did not need just any man.
I needed to trust, to admire, to desire.

Today, after five years
 of sleeping in your arms,
waking to the quiet
of our morning coffee,
wanting your opinion
about politics, films and books
not always agreeing, but always respecting,
knowing every word you speak
comes from your truth,
I dread the idea of ever living alone
without you.

# Gratitude

Here we are,
you and I
at rest on the peak,
the long climb behind us,
years of struggle
to discover:
*who are we?*

Would you go back,
be young again,
pursue your career,
raise your children to adults,
endure the pain
to feel the joy?
I would not,
not for a second.

My climb is mine
as yours belongs to you.
Every choice we made
along the way:
    our friends in common,
    our shared widowed life,
    our desire for love,
    all that brought us together
    and led us to this place.

Let us cherish the moment,
while we are able
then let us let go
without asking for more.

# Credo

Within my speck of time
from birth to death,
every choice I make
matters, yet chance
plays a role,
all my thoughts and actions
should be weighed for truth,
every word I speak will exist
in generations to come,
every kindness I offer
sends forth light in the universe.
I am resilient as a tree,
yet vulnerable as a reed,
the energy of my Spirit, formed
before I was born, will live
forever when I am gone.

# Acknowledgments

The following appeared, in slightly different forms, in the following journals.

"The House of Eighty": *The Louisville Review*
"Southern Cross": *The Dead Mule School of Southern Literature*

My first debt of gratitude for my love of poetry belongs to all the poets that have touched my life: A. A. Milne, Emily Dickinson, W. B. Yeats, Pablo Neruda, C. P. Cavafy, Wislawa Szymborska, Edna St. Vincent Millay, Rainer Maria Rilke, Derek Wolcott, W. S. Merwin, Stanley Kunitz, and Mary Oliver. And to all the poets whose work and workshops have influenced and inspired me to write my own: Molly Peacock, Jeffrey Harrison, Billy Collins, Dorianne Laux, and Wesley McNair; never to underestimate the value of the summer 2024 workshop in hopeful preparation for the publication of this chapbook led by Richard Blanco and including my dear poet friends Peggy Watson and Lucinda Ziesing.

For the past twenty years, my membership in the Live Poets' Society of Boca Grande, our monthly meetings, our discussions of poetry in general and the critiques of my work has been an enjoyable and valuable experience. Special appreciation to the current members, Candy Hooper, Lindsay Major, Nancy White, Bobbie Marquis, Simonetta Balzer, and John Thomas. Other vital encouragement has come from my insightful readers, Carol Sundberg, Lucinda Sullivan, Nan Carey and, of course, my children, Eleanor Mallory, Grace Ott, and Charles Bingham, and my beloved partner David Mumford.

I am certain that nothing in my writing life will ever equal the joy I felt from receiving Sena Jeter Naslund's Thanksgiving 2024 note praising my poems in *Daffodils in December* and offering publication by Fleur-de-Lis Press. Working on production of this chapbook with her talented and brilliant daughter Flora K. Schildknecht has been an honor and a pleasure. I could not have asked for a more creative book designer than Jonathan Weinert. It is particularly meaningful to me that the cover image was designed by my granddaughter-in-law Haley Manin Ott.

In my late eighties, the satisfaction of seeing my poems blossom from emotional seeds of experience to a garden of words on a page in such an esteemed publication has been the fulfillment of my most daring dreams.

# About the Author

**Alice Bingham Gorman** is a writer of fiction, nonfiction, and poetry. She earned an MFA in Writing from Spalding University in 2005 and received an Honorary PhD in Fine Arts from the Memphis College of Art in 2001. Her writing has been published in *Vogue, O, the Oprah Magazine, O's Little Book of Love and Friendship, The Louisville Review*, and countless regional periodicals and art publications. Born and raised in Memphis, Tennessee, she now divides her time between Maine and Florida. She is the author of the novel *Valeria Vose*.

Photo by Patricia Christakos

# About Fleur-de-Lis Press

In 1996 Fleur-de-Lis Press was launched to celebrate twenty years of continuous publication of *The Louisville Review*. From its start in 1976, *TLR* has fostered the development of new writers. An early poem by Alberto Riós now appears in standard literature textbooks, and *TLR* published the work of Louise Erdrich while she was a student at Johns Hopkins. Other notable contributors include Jhumpa Lahiri, Tony Hoagland, Stephen Dunn, Claudia Emerson, and Ursula Hegi.

Since receiving the Kentucky Arts Council's award for the best literary magazine in the state with its first issue, the goal of *The Louisville Review* continues to be to import the best writing to local readers, to export the best local writers to a national readership, and to juxtapose the work of established writers with new writers.

Named to celebrate the life of Founding Editor Sena Jeter Naslund's mother, Flora Lee Sims Jeter, Fleur-de-Lis Press publishes first books by writers published in *The Louisville Review* and by winners of *TLR*'s National Poetry Book Contests. Fleur de-Lis Press has published over twenty titles with endorsements by renowned authors including Maura Stanton, Maxine Kumin, Billy Collins, Tim O'Brien, Mark Doty, Melissa Pritchard, Silas House, and Fred Chappell.

*Daffodils in December: Poems from an Unexpected Life*, by Alice Bingham Gorman, is the first chapbook to be published by Fleur-de-Lis Press. The Louisville Review Corporation is a 501(c)(3) nonprofit literary organization and a proud member of the Community of Literary Magazines and Presses.

Fleur-de-Lis Press is named to celebrate the life
of Flora Lee Sims Jeter
(1901–1990)